My Vows to Love

A Poetry collection by Akimana Divine

"My vows to love is a splendid collection. The verses echo the title of the collection. It is a fascinating one suitable for any Lover of Literature and general reader"

- Micheal Mwangi Macharia, Reviewer

"You are all the love the world needs to survive, share it, be it, teach and feel it."

-Akimana Divine

"Love is an untamed force. When we try to control it, it destroys us. When we try to imprison it, it enslaves us. When we try to understand it, it leaves us feeling lost and confused."

– Paulo Coelho

Contents

Forward

Love was – still is a mystery. Renowned writers wrote about it, yet love refused to fit in the words of humans. It refused to be covered wholly. Two centuries and two decades have passed, and we are still penning about it. This collection is comprised of the poems that speak about love in different shades: some are light, some are heavy, and some are a blend of both. I admired the thorough expression with which this collection was written. It is a beautiful read that I am convinced one can have a myriad of emotions, even those one has never thought it was possible to feel. I believe that is due to the compelling power of poetry. It breaks down any topic even love that is so gigantic until a person can find the piece that expresses their feelings so exquisitely.

I have come to realize that love is one sacred topic that we all have a lot to talk about, the one part that makes us vulnerable. This collection contains love itself.

Sandra Nadege,

Author of 'First Creation and Light in the Dark'

Part I: Romance.

Blossoming Love

"A flower cannot blossom without sunshine, and a man cannot live without love."

- Max Muller

My Vows to Love

I can't promise you forever;

Only God can give it to us.

I promise to try to be and do better,

As long as air pumps through my lungs.

I promise to love you even when I am mad,

To listen to you even when the truth hurts,

And forgive you every time.

My love for you is greater than any mistake.

I promise to communicate better,

To confide in you every little secret,

To hold your hand when climbing gets harder

And makes you want to give up.

I promise to be your pillow to cry on,

Your shoulder to lean on when tears run dry;

When you need a place to lay your head on

And rest your mind.

I wish I could promise you eternity,

Because heaven might feel lonely without you,

But even when I or you go,

Rest assured that your love is tattooed on my soul.

Here is the promise that I am sure of;

I will laugh at your jokes even when I am mad at you,

And I will support you.

This, I vow to you sweet love.

His Charms

He charmed his way through my heart,

With his smile and time that he gave me.

His consistence kicked my stubbornness out of the way;

My heart opened like an abandoned house.

I poured my mind and soul into his,

I sank deeper like salt in water,

I gave his life a delicious taste.

Consistence short-lived my hunger for love;

My heart cracked faster than it opened up.

Tears became my pillow's best friend,

Nights became long,

Aches found a room in my heart,

But still, I loved again.

Before Dawn

It's seven in the evening,
I don't want to be alone in this bed;
It's cold and dull.

I want to be held so tight,
Not to feel my anxieties.
I want to feel my lips touched.

I can pretend that I don't feel lonely,
But I don't want to.
A sister needs to be felt and had.

I want to wake up in someone's arms,
And it is dawn and I can't remember
Hours between seven and dawn

I want to watch the sun rise,
Feeling your breath on my neck,
With your arms around my waist

Between The Sheets

Entice my neck with your lips,

Lick my ear with your tongue,

Let your lips glide against mine;

Sensually without friction,

As your fingers entice my nipples.

Let your warm tongue slide

Between these heavy melons;

These dark nipples are as hard as your horny look.

Let your lips trace along the path,

That leads to your promised land.

I'm so wet and horny for you;

Come and hold my waist tightly,

Put your tongue in me,

Feel me wining on it,

As I beg you to pound me hard.

Dear Future Husband

Dear future husband,

Forgive me; so many times I have said,

That love doesn't exist,

But that was the hurt talking,

Because I know you are out there.

Dear future husband,

If you are out there as I hope,

I hope you are happy with your life.

Even without me, live.

Dear future husband,

Being single is fun and liberating,

But I am waiting for you

Like how a girl waits for her periods;

Anxious, nervous but happy

Dear future husband,

I forgive you for taking so long to arrive,

But I am grateful and restful,

Knowing that you are out there looking for me

Handsome Stranger

His scent rushed through my nose,
My eyes could not turn away.

I prayed that wind blow him my way,
But the sun got jealous.

His smile gave me Goosebumps.
The moment I stood across him,
I held my chest.

I begged the moon to glow lighter,
For me to look at him clearer;
All true, he was all that.

His voice sent my soul to its knees;
It begged for the stars to lay light on his heart.

Before I could speak,
He held my arm and asked me,
"Is this yours, miss?"

My scarf smelled like him for a week;

I was scared to wash it,

Unsure if I will meet him again.

To My Soul Searcher

I have been looking for you too,
Just know that I am searching.

I have signed up to every application,
Just to look for you.

I have made a ton of mistakes in search for you,
And that's okay because I learned from them.

I am sorry that it is taking too long,
But I am getting ready for you.

Don't give up yet, I know how hard it is.
Heartbreaks are exhausting but you are almost here.

I can't promise to give you my whole heart;
It has been shattered into pieces.

I am not worried for your love;
It will tape my heart back into a beautiful piece.

I can promise you that wherever you are passing,

Finding you will only belong in time – not in mind.

Soul mate, keep coming if you exist,

I am here just across the finish line.

Forbidden Love

He is the forbidden apple,
The Hollywood eye candy

He is the KFC of my desires,
His age is as light as his presence.

I like his firm arms around me,
Until guilt kicks in

His lips on my skin,
Are the sleeping pills that I need to last

The world is still in the moment;
The clock stops in his chest.

The actions are loud enough,
For both our silence

I feel fifteen;
That's a good feeling that make me last.

I feel easy as the sun in winter,

I can stay in the bubble forever.

His strokes feel like 'weed highs';

I can feel depression freeing.

Don't tell me there is a hurricane,

I don't want to leave this fairytale.

"You call it madness, but I call it love."

- Don Byas

Heartbeat

My heart beats for you,

My mind thinks of you,

My eyes smile for you,

Each of your word warms my soul.

My heart dances with joy,

You give me strength to live,

Without you my knees are weak,

Before you, depression lived within.

You cheer me up in dullness,

You belong with me,

You give me butterflies,

Every time you walk by.

Loving you is as simple as reading a book,

You make me shy even when you are miles away,

As you stare right through my soul.

Thank you for loving me.

Thinking of You

With you in my mind, I feel calm.

Sadness finds no room;

I feel complete by just thinking of you.

World's pleasure has no place

In my heart anymore

I feel you in every vessel.

My nights are shorter,

Now that I have you to dream about,

I wish the moon would stay.

Dear Boyfriend

Dear boyfriend,

Your love makes me feel more beautiful,

Your confidence in me gathers my pieces.

Dear boyfriend,

Your joy is mine,

Your sorrows shatter my soul into pieces,

And I tear down.

Dear boyfriend,

I feel an undiluted and genuine love for you.

Your kindness puts my soul to my knees;

I adore you.

Dear boyfriend,

You bring every poetic and lyrical word out of me;

I want to scream to the world that I love you.

Purity

Airport is the last place,

I hoped to meet my other half

But our reaction when we did,

Gave me a wave of hope

When he saw me,

His reaction was a smile;

Shy enough to trigger my curiosity,

And warm enough to make mine copy it.

He asked if he could help me with my luggage;

All I could see was his eyes full of kindness.

I knew that the rest of my life,

Was going to be brighter and joyful

He asked my name,

But I was already miles away to our honeymoon.

The next five minutes, a family was complete;

I wrote my heart away in his phone.

Poetry became my new language,

His love became the trigger of my creativity,

In his presence, I knew peace and purity.

My Happy Place

I don't want to be here,

It's piecing my ears drum,

But I don't care because you are here.

With you, things feel better.

I have muted all the noises;

All I want to hear is your sweet whisper,

With that soft tone

I want to run away from this crazy place,

But I won't.

Your arms are holding me tight;

I feel safe.

Have I told you how much I love you,

And how safe and happy you make me feel?

With you, I can take over the world

Hello Love

Love,
I promise to never give up
Searching for you

Love,
Disappointments will never
Come between you and me.

Love,
I will look for you in every living soul
Until I find you.

Love,
My faith in you
Runs deeper than Lake Tanganyika

Love,
Wounds may slow me down
But they will never put me down forever.

Love,

We may have had a rocky start

But our bond is beyond human sight.

Love,

Mend my bleeding soul

As I search for a mate to share you with.

Love,

Promise me that if I stop looking for you

You will find me.

Love,

As I stay on this journey

Kindly find a way to visit this bleeding world

Little Things

It is the sound our lips make when you kiss me,
The feeling your tongue sends to my soul.

It is the butterflies in my belly,
When you come close and hold my hands.

It is the bliss in my chest,
When you call me and say,
"Everything will be okay."

It is the way you laugh at my jokes
That none else gets —
And we, laughing at them
For not getting our jokes

It is the little promises you keep,
Even when it is hard
It is the little things that tell me,
How ready we are for this.

Marriage Not Wedding

Kiss me passionately every day-
Like you did on our wedding day

Recite your vows to me every morning-
As you cuddle and hold me tight safely.

Love and forgive me even on our worst-
Day as you did when paradise couldn't define us.

Fight with me all you want but keep in mind that
We are in this for all and no mistake is greater than US.

Walking down the aisle was a great honour but-
Being married to you is the greatest gift from God.

The heart is the only broken instrument that works.

-    T.E. Kalem.

Broken Vows

My first love got married,

I don't know how to take the news.

He promised forever;

Now it flew away as fast.

Funny, right?

"I swear to you baby,

I will take care of your heart."

He swore to his knees,

As he begged for his first kiss.

But again, he probably was horny.

"Trust me, baby, you are the only girl for me;

I will always love you."

His phone calls were convincing.

I recall his constant visits with endless gifts,

And ear-capturing conversations.

Nights under the moon,
Carelessly kissing all night long,
Lying in the grass uncaring about the cold;
With him, warmth came along.
His love was a blanket;
With him, I felt blessed.

He had me wrapped around his finger;
I forgot to protect my little heart.
For a second he filled a hole
My broken family had dug out.
I hope he takes care of her,
The way he didn't do to me.

Fading Away

I have felt you slipping off my heart,
Like a bad fat,
After one drinks an apple cider.

I have travelled miles just to feed my desperate soul,
And yet my hungry mind still demands,
To check on your selfishness.

You have promised heaven on earth –
In the name of love and yet I still see the birds;
Flying under it and all my hopes.

I am afraid to call it love,
Because as I know it, love never fades away;
These feelings are being washed away.

Don't get me wrong,
Your desire to me is floating,
Your rotting heart needs a threat to hold on,
But a girl has to move on.

"You can spend minutes, hours, days, weeks, or even months over-analysing a situation; trying to put the pieces together, justifying what could've, would've happened… or you can just leave the pieces on the floor and move on."

- Tupac Shakur

Feeling Indifferent

Indifference, I feel,

Not fun, I feel like water.

You chose someone else;

I hope it made you happy.

I gave and gave some more,

I tried to win your love from my gut,

And I **didn't** surrendered

Your name became my ringtone.

My soul and mind, I submitted,

But still, I wasn't enough for you to stay.

I understand that I had no place

In your heart and mind.

I heard that you are doing well,

I am glad you found happiness,

I am here wishing that I made you

As happy as you look where you are.

I am angry to myself,

For I have trusted you with my whole heart,

Knowing that you were just a human,

Who could break it into pieces and throw it.

I Am Okay

Every time you ask me how I am doing,

I realize that you expect a sad response.

I say that I am okay,

Just to ease the pain.

Sometimes, I say that I am okay,

To persuade myself to be okay,

So that I can start to feel what to say,

Since alcohol and movies do not work.

Friends, I tell you that I am okay,

Hoping that you notice I am not.

If you know me well,

You would know that to me,

Okay is when my eyes smile as big as my lips.

To the unattached, I say that I am okay.

It is a reflex;

They are just asking for the sake of politeness.

I see no need to waste their energy,

Saying that I am not okay.

Most times I say that I am okay,

To make you peaceful,

Which doesn't worry me more –

Stress and depress me than I already am,

Or take away the little okay

I have been working on.

I Miss You

How I wish you were here!

I am holding your pictures,

Staring and tearing them up;

It hurts to miss you.

I never knew how much

I will need you by my side;

Now I wish that I have spent

Every waking up moment with you.

The world feels empty;

I hear my voice ringing back to me.

I cannot even send a prayer skyward;

I feel stuck in an elevator.

See me and hold me in your arms,

The thought of comfort in your mind helps a little,

But you know my wish;

You shouldn't have left me – I miss you.

My Love Song

I miss us watching the moon glow,

I miss laying my head on your shoulder,

I miss the sweet taste of your lips.

I went back home in your shirt;

I miss your smell **and arms** wrapped around me,

As I hold myself in bed.

The small nothings we laughed at;

I miss the late-night walks with you,

As we laughed at strangers making out.

Being comfortable while sitting in the silence,

Laying your head on my laps,

Smiling in your sleep;

I miss these small nothings.

Shirt

I have been looking at your shirt;
All I see is you pulling it out.
It is stuck on your head;
We laugh at it as I pull it off.

I remember you giving me your shirt,
And the next morning when I woke up in it,
As fresh as a ripe tomato.

I hold it close to my chest,
It still smells like you – I swear.
I am torn between washing it and sleeping in it again.

Do I give it away?
Oh no! That would erase how you made me feel,
And the time you loved me as if I was your muse.

Once In Love with You

I always wonder why

I am falling in love with you.

This much, I feel,

And this less I know why.

Does your heart beat or it's motionless?

I can't feel your pulse yet,

But I dream of our heartbeat rhyming.

Haven't you loved before?

Can I teach you how to love me?

Just express yourself in your love language,

I will listen closely.

Are you in love with someone else?

I wonder because as I know love,

It needs no degree in literature,

But yet you make it sound like mechanical engineering.

I pray and wish that you are honest with me,

I might be in love with you this much,

But I can learn to live without you,

And tell you in tails of 'Once in love with you'

The Skin We Lose

Every time I think of intimacy,
I feel the pain I felt when they decide
To take my sensitivity.

I am scared of feeling nothing at all;
What if I don't experience what the first time is,
Or even the times to come.

You took away my right to choose,
How my body should be shaped,
And destroyed me with your rigid norms.

You took away my womanhood,
But you won't be there when I painfully scream,
From my body to soul.

I loved and love every tight and loose skin;
The disgust you grow when you look at me,
Motivates me to adore my whole.

Part II: Friendship

"Life is partly what we make it, and what it is made by the friends we choose."

- Tennessee Williams

Kindness

You can sing to me,

You can call me every day,

And buy me everything,

You think I need;

You can dress me well,

Make me smell like lavender,

Open doors for me,

And pull a chair out for me to see your gentleness;

You can pray with me,

Or pray for me,

But if your actions don't reflect kindness,

You are a stranger.

My Forever Friend

Hey friend,

It has been a minute since you and I talked like this.

I have been texting you and sending letters,

Hoping that you will reply back.

The other day,

I held your picture in my arms,

And all the memories rushed to me.

I remembered our jokes and plans,

To adopt a child together, be co-parents,

And travel the world together.

The distance never made any difference,

We talk like there are no miles between us.

You made me smile as much as you did,

The first day I came for a visit;

We cooked and played guitar.

People tell me that it's not healthy to write to you,

But if I stop, that will mean that you are truly gone.

Our memories can't allow me to accept that,

Especially the nights you came to me,

And let me ramble all my crazy dreams and ideas

Which you always said, "Keep going, gal. I got you."

"When you lend an ear, you earn a heart."

- Sandra Nadege

Library Love

It's the old ink smell that I love;

The smell of old books,

That gives me hope for literature.

It's the safety of my sanity,

That I feel as soon as I go inside.

It's the joy on my face.

It's the respect in tones of people,

Who undermine the minds within.

It's the imagination of a thousand brilliant minds —

Under one roof; and the peace it gives me.

It's the hope for the kept history,

To secure the future and dreams for the young.

It's a hospital for ignorance,

A company of the lonely souls,

The solitude for introverts.

Angel

She is real in nature,

A born again sinner with a sweet melody.

Her hard-to-get treat pulls many,

Her silence is her soul's shield.

Intelligence is her survival kit,

In this ignorant and sad world.

She believes many but admires a few,

Her soulful smile is the sadness pill.

Her joy is contagious like her generosity,

Her warm hugs heal anxieties.

Powerfully Delicate

The beginning of life she is,

She lives in you and me;

She is you and you are her.

She is the world's greatest treasure,

Only humans can sense from a distance.

She is a diamond **in mud,**

She fears no pain whatsoever;

She stands on thorns for beauty.

She breaks her hips,

And tears her body to give life;

Her breasts are stretched and bitten to feed you.

She is a goddess,

She deserves to be loved and honoured.

For delicacy is your power plate,

Fall to her feet and let her love bless you.

Open Book

History, we find,
Antic love, she gives.

Adventurous, she is,
Fantasy is her other name.

Hope, she instils in you;
Healing is her Mojo.

Having her is,
The greatest gift to yourself.

Wondrous words, you find;
Literacy, she provides.

Unbutton her;
Anything, you will find.

She will fight your demons;
Her bliss will be yours.

She is a secret harmless friend

That you need.

Part III: Parental Love

"A parent's love is whole no matter how many times divided."

- Robert Brault

Natural Love

I am surrounded by people,
But only you can make me feel special.

In your presence, anger disappears –
Like the grey mist at the touch of sunrise,
You make me feel safe again.

Your hugs are so warm;
They heal my wounded soul,
And straighten my bent bones.

Your laughter quenches my thirsty soul,
Sends me joy and brightens my day.

Giving birth to you was,
The most opt decision I ever made

God's Love

Loving and forgiving, you are.

Sunday school taught me,

That you are omnipresent.

The God I believe is a father,

A brother, a friend, a counselor,

A shoulder to lean on in absence of strength.

The God I believe in is not bitter,

Like how some Christians describe Him.

He doesn't plan to burn his creations.

The God father I believe in,

Doesn't need you to scream to the walls,

For Him to hear you out.

He listens to your heartbeats and works miraculously.

He is not an angry or confusing God

Like what religions teach us.

He is love and I am his;

What will I lack?

God Father

Your perfection covers my imperfections,

I worry not for I know,

That I work with a mighty king.

God father,

I know your love is beyond my weakness,

Your protection guards and heals my broken heart.

God father,

I come to you in full transparency;

Allow me to repeat myself,

Maybe you will remember me.

God father,

I lay my life in your hands,

For you have moulded it.

You know better how to handle and guide me.

Dear Mother

Dear mother,

Thank you for giving up on your youth,

To give me life and nurse me to growth.

Dear mother,

Thank you for standing firm and being an example

Of what a strong woman looks like.

Dear mother,

Thank you for educating me and showing me

Connections are just additions to hard work.

Dear mother,

Thank you for infinite unconditional love

That you give me every day.

"The world is full of broken souls walking on endless pain, we need love now more than ever."

"Finding love is all heart break, disappointment and

Misery until it isn't."

"You know you truly love someone when you still love them in lack of intimacy, trust and respect, that's the forever we vow to"

"When you feel like giving up on the person you

Vowed to love forever, remember that love

Forgives, love is patient and love is beyond

Any paper you think tied you to your partner."

"When you feel like LOVE is dead around you,

Be the love your surroundings needs to rekindle."

My moonlight in the dark

You held my hand across the dark valleys

When the depth of fear held my feet in the mud.

You made my soul dance when pain sucked life-

Out of me, you promised to make me laugh-

The rest of my life and cry with me.

Reason to love you

I love you because you make me laugh,

I love you because you shine brighter for-

Both of us when my light run short.

I love you because you see me,

I love you because you remind me how beautiful

I am when my mind is playing tricks on me.

I love you because my face lights up when I see you

I love you because you push me to be my best self and

Most of all, I love for showing every part of you, the

scary and the joyful parts.

"Love is like the wind, you can't see it but you can feel it."

– Nicholas Sparks

I think of you

I think of you and my mind is calm

Suddenly, my world is complete and

Boredom loses a room in my heart.

The pleasure of every other living means

Nothing no more and the humdrum life stays-

With the non-spiritual beings.

My prayer for you my Love

I pray for the heavens to bless the soil you walk on,

I pray to God for blessing every life you touch,

I pray for overflowing blessings up on your life.

I pray for your heart to know no agony,

I pray to God to give more love in your heart,

I pray for God's favour to follow you every day.

I pray for peace, health, security, empathy, sympathy,

I pray to God that He listens to you day and night,

I pray for your eyes to know no sorrow.

I pray for our children, their children and the Generation

After to know no poverty, to want nothing, be the peace

of the earth and beyond and to be the salt of the world.

How I know that we shall be okay

I dream of our forever to be eternal,
I mean in life and after that for death to-
Have no choice but accept our vows.

I dream of our memories to be the text-
Books for every generation to learn what-
Love is and for our light to be the brightest.

I pray for us to be our own best friends,
To rely on one other, to synch every-thought,
Feelings and to unite when things fall apart.

I know we shall be okay because as I pray for us,
I know you are praying for us and I fall in love with
You all over again knowing that you want as much.

Dear Angel

Your perfect imperfections only
Pull me closer to you.
You have shown me that love require
No shield for your kindness cover me.

Dear angel, I feel your love as much
As I see it and hear it from the warmth
Of your heart across mine.

The rhythm of your heartbeat communicates
With my soul and I know that you are my-
Guardian angel and I set for life.

Dear son

Dear son, when the world tells to be scared,
I want you to it in the eyes and tell it that-
You know who your God is and He is the mighty.

Dear son, I want you to grow know that you stronger
Than your fears, kinder than the ruthless world and
You wear your humanity to your sleeve.

Dear son, when you stand in the mirror see a beautiful,
Handsome, intelligent, caring, creative, smart, prayer
warrior, humane and a gentleman B'coz everything I see.

Dear son, I want you to know that you matter beyond all
earthly treasures, your life is valued, your contribution to
the world is beyond human sight so let your mind know.

Dear son, live like a king but serve your community like
a servant, speak your mind, let the mountains and valleys
feel your God given gifts, bless nations.

Baby boy

I want you to know that, you are my strength
You are most treasured God given gift.

Son, you feel my heart with overflowing joy
Your make my mornings brighter and my nights warm

Son, you are my inspirations for the days to come
You make the future seem brighter.

Son, I pray to God that I am only a vessel for the
Your purpose on and for God to give all the tools to be.

Note to self

Baby girl, you are beautiful,
You are intelligent and smart
You are worth more than earthly treasures.

Darling self, when you across these streets,
I want you to walk like you belong to this world
Just like everybody else.

Dear self, hold your chin up and sing the songs of
Praises to yourself as you look at those chic bones,
Those beautiful eyes and that wonderful mind.

Love, recite to yourself your worth, your contribution
To this world, always remember than you are more than
 Mere snack, you are a whole meal and let them know.

Sweetheart, you are as limited as you let your mind
Tell you and keep in mind that you hold the keys to
Your mind lock, I see and appreciate you.

www.ingramcontent.com/pod-product-compliance
Lightning Source LLC
Chambersburg PA
CBHW051449150726
48000CB00005B/2320